BUILDING BASIC
Reading
Skills

INFERENCE
LEVEL F

Dr. Thomas G. Gunning

ISBN 0-8454-1600-6
Copyright © 1998 The Continental Press, Inc.

CONTINENTAL PRESS
Elizabethtown, PA 17022

CONTENTS

Making Inferences About Feelings

Authors don't tell you everything in a story. They might not tell you, for instance, that a character is happy. But they show the character laughing and singing. It's up to you to infer how the person is feeling. You can make the inference because you know how people act when they are happy. As you read the following selections, make inferences about the main character in each one. Try to figure out how the character is feeling.

Read each story. Underline the correct answer to each question.

The audience was filled with important people, including the mayor, the police chief, and the fire chief. The police chief told the crowd the story. Hundreds of citizens searched the woods last week for a lost child. For hours, they had walked and looked and called her name. When it got dark, the searchers began to lose hope. But then, Keith Hanson, a young man from town, found the child huddled in a small cave. The little girl was soon reunited with her joyful parents. Keith's picture was on the front page of the town newspaper. He was interviewed on television. Now the police chief is giving Keith a medal.

How does Keith feel?

A. proud B. angry C. afraid D. disappointed

The answer is *A*. After finding the child, being on TV and in the newspaper, and being honored by important people, Keith would most likely feel proud. Answers *B, C,* and *D* are not correct. There was no reason for Keith to feel angry, afraid, or disappointed.

• •

Marilyn was sure she would get 100% on the spelling test. She had studied her list of words for nearly an hour the night before. She had even gotten up extra early the day of the test so she could go over the words once more. When it came time to take the test, Marilyn discovered she had studied the wrong words. She tried her best, but she only knew about half of the correct list.

How did Marilyn feel when she was taking the test?

A. confident B. stubborn C. upset D. tired

The answer is *C*. If Marilyn studied the wrong words and was doing badly on the test, she would most likely feel upset. *A, B,* and *D* are not correct. Marilyn wouldn't feel confident because she realized she studied the wrong words. There is no reason for her to be stubborn, and the story doesn't suggest she was tired.

Teaching Lesson: Inferring Feelings

Read each story. Underline the correct answer to each question.

Just as he turned the corner, Sam spotted Honey Bear. Honey Bear was the biggest, meanest watchdog Sam had ever seen. Honey Bear was usually chained up, but somehow the dog had broken loose. Honey Bear was walking towards Sam, snarling every step of the way. Oh no! Honey Bear was now running towards him, his huge fangs flashing in the sunlight.

Just then Sam heard his mom, "Sam, wake up. It's seven o'clock. You'll be late for school."

"Oh, wow!" said Sam. "What a nightmare that was!"

How did Sam feel when he woke up?

    A. ashamed   B. tired   C. relieved   D. confused

• •

Shawna stopped at the store to buy some bread and a gallon of milk. She went to a check-out counter and put her things on the moving belt. The cashier picked up the bread and held its Universal Product Code over a beam of light. A computer read the code. The price, $1.29, flashed on the register. At the same time a strange-sounding voice said, "Bread—$1.29." Shawna looked at the cashier, but the cashier's lips weren't moving. Then Shawna heard a voice saying, "Gallon of milk—$2.49." The cashier saw the funny look on Shawna's face and explained that the store had just bought a talking cash register. That way customers could hear the price as well as see it.

How did Shawna feel when she first heard the voice?

    A. surprised   B. angry   C. amused   D. impatient

• •

The two main islands of New Zealand are separated by a narrow passage of water. Ships passing through Cook Strait face extremely rough waters. Long ago, ships had a guide to lead them safely through the hazardous strait. That guide was a dolphin named Pelorus Jack.

In 1888, the captain of a ship caught sight of Pelorus Jack leaping high into the air. The curious captain followed the dolphin through the dangerous passage. Pelorus Jack guided hundreds of ships through Cook Strait over the next twenty-four years. The dolphin disappeared in 1912 and was never seen again.

How do you think most people felt when Pelorus Jack disappeared?

    A. angry   B. sad   C. lonely   D. relieved

Read each story. Underline the correct answer to each question.

James Ritty was on a ship traveling across the Atlantic Ocean when he spotted a device attached to the ship's propellers. The device counted and kept track of the number of times the propellers turned. Ritty looked closely at the counter. He asked many questions about it. He then began to imagine a machine that would keep a record of the money put into it.

By November 4, 1879, James Ritty had invented the first cash register. His first machine made some mistakes. But Ritty had an accurate one by the next year.

How did James Ritty feel when he saw the counting device on the ship?

    A. bored   B. interested   C. irritated   D. surprised

• •

Alicia ate very little lunch. It was difficult to eat when her stomach was doing flip-flops. Alicia looked at her watch. In just ten minutes, she would be giving a speech to the whole school. There would be six hundred pairs of eyes peering at her and six hundred pairs of ears listening to every word. What if she forgot what she wanted to say? Alicia's mouth felt dry. Her legs began to quiver.

How does Alicia feel?

    A. disappointed   B. proud   C. hungry   D. nervous

• •

Brenda Donaldson did not go to work Monday. She had a bad cold and was home in bed. Brenda was reading ads in the morning paper when she stopped and read one ad a second time. She wanted to be certain she read it correctly. Sure enough, there was a job advertisement for people with colds. It paid $80 a day.

Brenda thought the ad was a joke. She dialed the phone number to find out. The job was for real. A scientist in Stamford, Connecticut, was studying colds. People would be paid $80 a day to sniff and sneeze while the scientist tried out different medicines to find the most effective ones.

How did Brenda feel when she read the ad?

    A. surprised   B. sleepy   C. greedy   D. unhappy

Inferring Feelings

Read each story. Write your answer to each question on the lines.

Army worms aren't worms at all. They are caterpillars. Later, they turn into moths. When the caterpillars get hungry, they join together in a row. This band is twelve to fourteen feet long and two to three inches wide. The caterpillars march in this way, looking for corn, grains, cotton, and other crops. Moving on, the army worms eat all the food in their path.

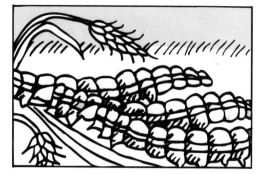

How would farmers feel if they saw army worms marching toward their fields?

_____

_____

_____

• •

While Su Li was tying her sneakers, one shoestring broke. She didn't let that bother her, however. Then at breakfast, she spilled juice on her new jeans. Su Li felt like screaming, but she didn't. As she was crossing the front lawn, she slipped and fell into a mud puddle. That did it! Su Li got up and yelled as loud as she could, "This is an awful day!"

How did Su Li feel after she fell into the mud puddle?

_____

_____

_____

• •

Jamie was worried sick. She had searched the whole apartment, but she couldn't find the book that she borrowed from the town library. She needed the book about snakes for a report. Besides, if she couldn't find the book, she would have to pay for it. When Jamie arrived at school, she reached into her desk. There was her book. The gloomy look on her face was replaced by a sunny smile.

How did Jamie feel when she found the book?

_____

_____

_____

Drawing Conclusions

When you read, you often have to take the information given and draw a conclusion from it. For example, if you read an article that lists the million-dollar salaries and the runs produced by some of baseball's superstars, you can probably conclude that these players are very valuable to their teams.

Read each article. Underline the correct answers.

Some plants protect themselves from animals by giving off a bad odor. One tropical tree smells like garlic. There is a poisonous plant that smells like a pile of rotting garbage. Other plants, such as poison ivy and poison sumac, give out a liquid that keeps animals away. A great many plants have thorns, spines, or stinging hairs that protect them. Still other plants keep safe by disguising themselves. The flowering stone is round and flat. It grows very close to the ground. A person would believe it really is a stone until she or he touched it or looked at it closely.

From the article, you can conclude that _____.

A. most plants are dangerous

B. most plants are not useful

C. plants protect themselves in various ways

D. most plants disguise themselves

The answer is C. The article tells how plants use odors, poisonous liquids, thorns, spines, and disguises to keep plant-eating animals away. These special features show that plants protect themselves in various ways. Answer A is not correct because the article doesn't suggest that most plants are dangerous. Answer B is not correct, for the article doesn't mention ways in which plants are useful. And answer D is not correct because the article does not suggest that most plants disguise themselves.

• •

Encyclopedias in book form present information in text, pictures, photographs, and maps. CD-ROM encyclopedias use recordings and films. Suppose you wanted to find out about John F. Kennedy. If you looked him up, you might see a film clip of President Kennedy and his family. You might also hear a recording of one of his speeches. Of course, there would also be an article giving the important points of Kennedy's life and presidency.

From the article, you can conclude that CD-ROM encyclopedias _____.

A. cost less

B. give the user a "you-are-there" feeling

C. are used mostly in schools

D. are not very popular

Teaching Lesson: Drawing Conclusions

Read each article. Underline the correct answer to each question.

One of the most famous collections of stories of all time is Aesop's fables. Chances are you've heard about the goose that laid the golden eggs or about the race between the tortoise and the hare.

It is believed that Aesop was a Greek slave who lived some 2,600 years ago. He enjoyed telling stories and made them popular. Some of the stories had probably been around a long time; others may have been created by Aesop. No one knows for sure.

Three hundred years after Aesop's death, a man named Demetrius Phalereus gathered together two hundred fables and put them in a collection with Aesop's name. Since then, other writers have put together different collections of Aesop's fables, adding some new ones or dropping some old ones.

From the article, you can conclude that _____.

    A. Aesop created most of Aesop's fables

    B. Aesop did not actually create any of Aesop's fables

    C. Demetrius made up most of Aesop's fables

    D. a number of people have taken part in creating Aesop's fables

• •

The human body needs about one teaspoon of salt a day. It is easy to get enough salt. In fact, for some people, the problem is getting too much salt.

If people want to cut back the amount of salt they eat, one thing they can do is stop shaking salt on their food. Since salt is already in many things we eat, people may need to eat less of these foods. Most pretzels and potato chips contain a lot of salt. People can taste it and even see it. Other foods, though, have salt we can't see and taste so easily. Some cereals, canned soups and other foods, frozen dinners, and cheeses have lots of salt. One bowl of some kinds of cereal has more salt than fourteen potato chips. The only way to be sure of the salt content is to check the ingredients listed on the label.

From the article, you can conclude that _____.

    A. all foods have some salt

    B. salt is in a surprising number of foods

    C. people who do hard work need more salt than those who don't

    D. most people don't get enough salt

Read each article. Underline the correct answers.

Jim Watt owns a gas station in Colville, Washington. Running a gas station is hard work, but Jim's dog, Tiger, helps out. If Jim needs a wrench or a screwdriver, Tiger gets it for him. When a customer pays with a check or paper money, Tiger carries it in his teeth to Jim. Tiger also helps keep the gas station clean by picking up stray pieces of paper and depositing them in the trash can. Tiger even helps out when Jim takes money from the station to the bank. The dog carries the money pouch in his teeth. The first time Tiger trotted into the bank to make a deposit, the teller's mouth flew open. She stared for a while, but now she's used to Tiger.

1. **From the story, you can conclude that Tiger is _____.**
   A. a smart dog
   B. an old dog
   C. a lazy dog
   D. a mean dog

2. **How did the teller probably feel the first time Tiger made a deposit?**
   A. impatient
   B. afraid
   C. surprised
   D. foolish

• •

Charlene put down her saw and reached for her hammer. She then drove three long nails into the tall post. After sawing three more boards approximately the same length, she nailed those boards next to the first one. All day long, Charlene nailed and sawed. By the end of the day, the frame for the walls and the roof was up. Charlene looked at it carefully. She smiled to herself when she saw how much work she had done and how well everything was going.

1. **From the story, you can conclude that Charlene is a _____.**
   A. plumber
   B. carpenter
   C. baker
   D. mechanic

2. **At the end of the day, Charlene felt _____.**
   A. pleased
   B. exhausted
   C. worried
   D. frustrated

Supporting Conclusions

Sometimes people draw hasty or false conclusions. This can happen if all the facts or details aren't considered. When you draw a conclusion, you should be able to back it up with facts or other details. In the following articles, you are given conclusions but asked to support them. That means you point out facts and details to back them up. As you read each of the articles in this section, think about the conclusion that is being drawn and how you might support or prove it.

Read the article. Then answer the question.

America's oldest organized sport is lacrosse. From the beginning, players used a stick with a net on the end to hurl a ball into a goal. The Iroquois and Algonquin played the game long before people from Europe came to North America. The game was called the "little brother of war."

When the Algonquin and Iroquois played the game, the teams were large. Each side could have as many as five hundred players. The goals were often as far apart as half a mile. The sport was fast moving and rough, but the native peoples viewed it as a good way to keep in shape.

How do you know lacrosse was played on a very large field? Underline two details.

   A. Each team could have five hundred players.

   B. Lacrosse is America's oldest organized sport.

   C. The game was a fast-moving one.

   D. The goals could be half a mile apart.

   E. The game was called the "little brother of war."

The answers are *A* and *D*. If each team had five hundred players, then the field would have to be large to have enough room for all those people. If the goals were half a mile apart, then the field would be very large. The name given to the game doesn't indicate the size of the field. Also, just because the sport is old or fast moving doesn't mean it was played on a big field.

Read each article. Write your answers to each question in the boxes.

How would you like to go to a school that's built on a beach and has a huge outdoor pool? Does it sound more like a hotel than a school? That's because it's both. Stonington Beach is a hotel run by people learning the hotel business. In classes in a nearby building, students learn how to make beds, cook dinner, and take reservations. After they've been to enough classes, they start working in the hotel. They sweep up, wait on tables, and work in the office. In fact, they spend more time working in the hotel than they do in class. After two years of school and work experience, the students are ready to begin their careers.

How do you know the students are well trained? On the lines, write two more details that prove, or back up, this conclusion.

CONCLUSION	PROOF
The students are well trained.	1. Students learn how to make beds, cook dinner, and take reservations. 2. _____ _____ 3. _____ _____

• •

Jamar has always had a special interest in any animal that lives in the sea. So when he had to do a report, he chose whales as his topic. He spent most of Monday and Tuesday afternoons getting information for his report on whales. On Tuesday night, Jamar spent three hours writing his report. He revised it on Wednesday night. Jamar checked the facts and rewrote two paragraphs that weren't clear. On Thursday night, he checked all the capitalization, punctuation, and spelling. Then he copied the report as neatly as he could on lined white paper.

How do you know that Jamar is a careful worker? On the lines, write two more details that prove, or back up, this conclusion.

CONCLUSION	PROOF
Jamar is a careful worker.	1. Jamar checked the facts in his report. 2. _____ _____ 3. _____ _____

Substantiating Conclusions

Read the article. Write your answers to the question in the box.

Smoke jumpers fight forest fires, speeding to them by airplane. The fire fighters then parachute to locations that would be difficult to reach in any other way. Becoming a smoke jumper isn't easy. A person must be an experienced fire fighter, with a knowledge of forests, and must pass a special test.

Linda Reimers had experience working on a fire fighting crew during three summer vacations. But she needed to pass the physical test held in May. Linda began preparing in November. She ran each day and lifted weights. When she got to the test, Linda was glad she was in shape. First, she had to run 1½ miles. Then Linda had to do many sit-ups, push-ups, and other exercises. Yet the hardest test was still to come. Linda had to dig fire ditches for fourteen hours. Linda Reimers passed the test and was on her way to being a smoke jumper.

How do you know that the physical test for smoke jumpers is difficult? On the lines, write <u>two</u> more details that prove this conclusion.

CONCLUSION	PROOF
The physical test for smoke jumpers is difficult.	1. Linda ran 1½ miles. 2. _____ _____ _____ 3. _____ _____ _____

Read the article. Write your answers to the question in the box.

For a number of years, TV shows were live. No one had invented a way to tape them. The problem was that it was difficult to record the sound and the video at the same time. Sound is recorded at one speed. However, video needs to be recorded at a much faster speed. It would have been necessary to use thousands of feet of tape just to record a few minutes of video. Charles Ginsburg and a team of inventors were put in charge of the problem. To deal with the differences in speed between audio and video signals, the team had to test out a number of devices, most of which didn't work. Finally, the team created a tape head that was able to pick up signals in two directions at one time.

Even though the signals traveled at different speeds, they were picked up in such a way that they were recorded and played back at the same time. But the picture was too fuzzy. At last, several years later, in 1956, Ginsburg and his team demonstrated their

Video Tape Recorder. It weighed more than a thousand pounds and was about three feet high and two feet wide, but it worked. Now, at last, TV programs could be taped and shown later. But one problem remained. The recorder had to be made smaller and cheaper.

How do you know that inventors of the Video Tape Recorder had to solve several problems? On the lines, write <u>two</u> more details that prove this conclusion.

CONCLUSION	PROOF
Inventors of the Video Tape Recorder had to solve several problems.	1. Sound and video have to be recorded at different speeds. 2. _____ _____ _____ 3. _____ _____ _____

Predicting Outcomes

Some conclusions are actually predictions. For instance, weather forecasters look at instruments and draw conclusions from the readings. Then they make a prediction about future weather. As you read the following articles, think about the information in them and the predictions you might make based on that information.

Read the articles. Underline the correct answers.

Mr. Hill was startled when the red bike zipped in front of his car. The rider hadn't stopped at the stop sign or even noticed the car coming up the road. "That girl is going to get hit if she doesn't obey the rules of the road," Mr. Hill said to himself. "Look at her. Now she's riding on the wrong side of the road." Just then the rider's hood slipped down. "Hey, that's my daughter Lila," Mr. Hill thought with surprise.

When Mr. Hill gets home, he will say to Lila, _____

A. "Your bike needs fixing."

B. "You'd better tie your hood tighter when you ride your bike."

C. "I thought you were in your room doing your homework."

D. "I want to talk to you about the way you ride your bike."

The answer is *D*. Even before he realized the rider was his daughter, Mr. Hill noticed how carelessly the girl rode her bike and was afraid she would get hurt. Since he knows the rider was his daughter, it is almost certain that Mr. Hill will talk to her about her unsafe bike riding.

• •

A sudden snowstorm caught the hunters by surprise. They were too far from camp to make it back. The younger hunter began to panic, but the older man hardly seemed worried. He explained that there were dozens of cabins stocked with food, clothing, and wood in that part of Alaska. The supplies were to be used by travelers or hunters in an emergency. If someone used them, the supplies were to be replaced as soon as possible. The older man had a map showing the cabins' locations, and there was one just half a mile away. By the time the men reached it, the snow was getting deep, and the temperature was dropping fast. There was plenty of food and wood in the cabin. By morning the snow had stopped, and the hunters knew they could easily get back to camp.

After the hunters reached their camp, they _____.

A. went home as quickly as they could

B. went back to the cabin to drop off some food and wood

C. went back to the cabin and left money for the supplies on the table

D. called their homes

Read the articles. Underline the correct answers.

The early 1960s marked the beginning of the U.S. space program. Since then, some new materials have been developed for use in spacecraft and space suits. Many of these special materials are now in everyday use by people on Earth, too.

One fabric is used in running shoes. It is very thin and prevents heat from building up. Runners' feet stay cool with shoes made of this material. Thousands of police officers wear vests made out of Kevlar. This fabric, which is supposedly tougher than steel, is used to make bulletproof vests. Thinsulate is a thin fabric that's ideal for winter clothing. The fabric keeps body heat in so that people feel warm. Yet the fabric is so thin that people can move around easily. Another tough fabric, PBI, does an outstanding job of keeping heat out.

PBI would most likely be used to make clothing for _____.

   A. fire fighters   B. mountain climbers   C. sky divers   D. football players

• •

Many blind people read books and articles written in braille. Braille is an alphabet code of raised dots. People "read" it with their fingers. Some legally blind people, though, do have some sight. They are able to read book printing if it is large enough.

A special television camera and set can be used to make the letters and numbers of printed material appear larger. The camera is placed over the print. Then it is adjusted to make the letters larger. The lines of large print are shown on the television screen.

Because of the special television camera and set, _____.

   A. some blind people will be able to switch from touch reading to sight reading

   B. braille will no longer be needed

   C. many blind people will be able to see their favorite television shows

   D. blind people will be able to make videos

Predicting Outcomes

Read the paragraphs below. Write the correct answer to each question on the line.

Renata spends hours drawing trees, animals, and people. In fact, she has always liked to draw. This year Renata started special art lessons, even though she is just twelve years old.

• • • • •

Everyone except Caroline panicked when Jason got a nosebleed on the playground. Caroline asked someone to get the nurse. In the meantime, she led Jason to a bench. When he was seated, Caroline had him lean forward. Then she carefully pressed the lower part of his nose.

• • • • •

Bart likes to know what's happening. He's the only one in his class who reads three newspapers each day and watches the evening news on television. Bart also likes to write. Whenever his class writes reports, Bart usually does very well.

Lamont is good at explaining things. One night, Andy had trouble with his math assignment. He called Lamont. Lamont carefully told Andy how to do the problem step-by-step. When Andy said he still had trouble understanding it, Lamont patiently explained the problem again.

• • • • •

What Valerie enjoys the most is camping in the forest with her family. Valerie loves the quiet and beauty of the woods. She also believes people should take care of the forest and the animals that live there.

• • • • •

When Enrico sees lumber, he never sees it as just a pile of boards. Enrico looks at lumber as a new fence, a bookcase, a table, or even a new home. With a few tools and some wood, he can make just about anything.

1. **Which person seems most likely to become a doctor or nurse?**

_____

2. **Which person seems most likely to become a newspaper reporter?**

_____

3. **Which person seems most likely to become a teacher?**

_____

4. **Which person seems most likely to become a carpenter?**

_____

5. **Which person seems most likely to become a forest ranger?**

_____

6. **Which person seems most likely to become an artist?**

_____

Inferring Causes and Effects

People are curious creatures who want to know why things happen. So it's important to know causes. For instance, once the cause of a disease is known, steps can be taken to prevent or cure it. As you read each article in this section, try to figure out the cause of the event or action.

Read each article. Underline the correct answer to each question.

For many years, stories were told about strange creatures that lived in Africa. They were large, standing six feet tall and weighing four hundred pounds. When the animals got angry, they roared and beat their chests. Many people laughed at the stories about these creatures, but more than a hundred years ago, Paul Du Chaillu set out for the rain forests of Africa in search of them. His trip was successful, and Dr. Du Chaillu brought home the fur and skeleton of one animal to show doubters. Some people, though, still didn't believe the creatures really existed. When other scientists and explorers also saw the hairy animals, people slowly became convinced that gorillas were real.

Why didn't people believe the creatures existed?
- A. The creatures lived in Africa.
- B. The creatures were unlike anything people knew about.
- C. The people didn't trust explorers.
- D. The explorers were not well known.

The answer is *B*. People had a hard time believing the creatures existed because they were so different from anything they knew about. Answers *A*, *C*, and *D* are not correct. The article doesn't indicate people had trouble believing the creatures were real because they lived in Africa or because they distrusted explorers. And the article doesn't say whether the explorers were well known.

• •

Etienne de Silhouette became head of the French treasury in 1759. France was at war then and needed money. De Silhouette raised taxes and tried to get the king and his ministers to spend less. Those affected by de Silhouette's policies said he was cheap. They even called any picture that was an outline or cutout a *silhouette* because it wasn't a full drawing. People thought the picture seemed cheap—just like de Silhouette.

Why did people dislike de Silhouette?
- A. He was selfish.
- B. He led the country into war.
- C. He raised people's taxes.
- D. He wasn't a very good artist.

Teaching Lesson: Inferring Cause/Effect Relationships

Read each article. Underline the correct answer to each question.

Lynx spiders are different from many other kinds of spiders because they don't spin webs. They live on plants and move around by jumping from leaf to leaf. Lynx spiders eat insects found on the plants. If lynx spiders live on green plants, they are green. If they live on woody plants, they are brown.

Why are lynx spiders difficult to find?

A. They are good jumpers.

B. They hunt insects.

C. They live in dark places.

D. They match the color of their surroundings.

. . . .

The heart of a giraffe is four times as powerful as a human heart. Its job is to pump the blood throughout the animal's huge body. A full-grown giraffe is about nineteen feet tall. Its neck may be six or seven feet long. That means a lot of the giraffe's blood has to be pumped uphill.

Why does a giraffe need a powerful heart?

A. It is very tall.

B. It lives in a hot climate.

C. It gets a lot of exercise.

D. It lives in mountainous areas.

. . . .

Scientists have discovered that many lizards shed their tails when they are attacked. Surprisingly, some of the tails continue to move. Scientists found that lizards whose unattached tails keep moving escape from their attackers more often than lizards whose tails remain still. The attackers usually pursue the moving tails.

Why do lizards whose unattached tails move have a good chance of escaping from attackers?

A. The lizards are faster than the attackers.

B. The moving tails frighten the attackers.

C. The attackers stop chasing the lizards for a time.

D. The tails are poisonous.

Inferring Cause/Effect Relationships

Read each article. Underline the correct answer to each question.

Children usually have their first set of teeth until they are six or seven years old. The twenty teeth in this set are called baby teeth. Underneath the baby teeth are the beginnings of thirty-two permanent teeth. As children grow, these permanent teeth grow also. At the same time, the roots of their baby teeth begin to dissolve. By the time the permanent teeth have fully formed, the roots of the baby teeth have dissolved completely. Then the baby teeth fall out and are replaced by the permanent ones.

Why do baby teeth fall out?

   A. They aren't as strong as permanent teeth.

   B. They wear out.

   C. The roots are gone.

   D. They get a lot of wear.

• •

What is the most crowded place in the world? It is a small territory near China called Macao (muh•KOW). Macao, a Portuguese territory until 1999, consists of a peninsula and two small islands. Altogether there are about 491,000 people living on six square miles. That means there is an average of 82,000 people for each square mile. The United States, by comparison, has around 70 people for each square mile.

Greenland, which is a province of Denmark, is the least crowded territory. On this island, there are only about 7 people for each 100 square miles. Greenland isn't very green, as its name might suggest. Most of this vast island is a frozen wasteland of ice.

Why do you think Greenland has so few people?

   A. It is an island and very hard to reach.

   B. It is a small country and only has room for a few people.

   C. People would have great difficulty living on most parts of the island.

   D. It costs a lot of money to live there.

Inferring Cause/Effect Relationships

Inferring Character Traits

There is an old saying that actions speak louder than words. As you read the articles in this section, think about each person's actions. Based on those actions, what can you infer about the person?

Read each article. Underline the word or phrase that best tells about the person.

Years ago, when Barbara McClintock told other scientists about her research, some just didn't understand her ideas. Others thought she was foolish. Working mostly by herself, Dr. McClintock had been growing corn for years. She mixed seeds of various kinds of corn together. When the corn was grown, she carefully examined the kernels to see how the color was affected. Through this research, Barbara McClintock discovered some of the factors that cause living things to change.

Although many scientists laughed at her work, Dr. McClintock continued her research. After about thirty years, science began to catch up with her. Scientists realized that

Barbara McClintock had been on the right track all along. Working alone, she had made some of the most important discoveries of the twentieth century.

Dr. Barbara McClintock seemed to be the kind of person who _____.

   A. was easily angered by the actions of others   C. did not have much patience

   B. relied heavily on the opinions of other people   D. had a lot of faith in herself

The answer is *D*. Even though many other scientists paid little attention to her work and even laughed at it, Dr. McClintock continued her research. She must have had faith in herself to keep working when so many others thought she was wasting her time. Answers *A*, *B*, and *C* are not correct. The article does not say that Dr. McClintock became angry. Nor does it indicate that she relied on other people's opinions. Barbara McClintock went on with her work even though others thought she was foolish. She also had a lot of patience. It says she worked on her experiments for many years.

Before setting out on the road through the desert, Luis carefully checked his car. He looked under the hood for leaks. Then he made sure the four tires and the spare had enough air. The trip was only two hundred miles, but Luis stored two large containers of drinking water in the trunk. He also took a compass, a first-aid kit, a tool kit, a battery-powered lantern, and emergency flares. Just before leaving, he called ahead to tell his friend he would be there in about five hours.

From his actions, you can tell that Luis is _____.

   A. afraid   B. selfish   C. cautious   D. impatient

Read each article. Underline the correct answers.

There was always something special about Juliette Gordon Low, founder of the Girl Scouts of America. As a child, she made sure that stray dogs and cats around the neighborhood had food to eat. Juliette, nicknamed Daisy, became concerned about the family cow one bitterly cold day. She was afraid it wouldn't keep warm enough. Daisy ran upstairs, pulled the blanket off her bed, and used it to cover the animal. Soon after, Daisy discovered that some poor children nearby didn't have enough clothes to keep them warm in the winter. She decided to do something about that and immediately started a group called Helping Hands. The group's purpose was to make clothing for needy children.

From her actions, you can tell that Daisy Low was _____.

A. silly   B. lonely   C. fearful   D. kind

Daisy Low divided her time between England and the United States after her husband died in 1905. While in England, she met Robert and Agnes Baden-Powell. Robert was the founder of the Boy Scouts. Agnes, Robert's sister, started a similar group for girls called Girl Guides. Daisy soon became interested in scouting. When she returned home to Savannah, Georgia, in 1912, Daisy started a troop of sixteen Girl Guides. The girls learned to tie knots, make candy, and camp in the woods. Daisy Low then organized troops around the country. In 1913, she changed the name from Girl Guides to Girl Scouts and set up a national headquarters in Washington, D.C. By 1915, there were 42,000 Girl Scouts, but Daisy still wasn't satisfied. She traveled and formed troops in other countries, even though she was in poor health. When Daisy Low died in 1927, she was called "the best Girl Scout of them all."

From her actions, you can tell that Daisy Low was _____.

A. old and cranky

B. hardworking and determined

C. interesting but forgetful

D. discouraged and angry

Inferring Character Traits

Read each selection. Write your answer to each question on the lines.

Squanto, a member of the Pawtuxet tribe, played an important role in American history. The Pilgrims reached the shores of Massachusetts in December 1620. After spending a harsh winter aboard their ship, the *Mayflower*, they founded a settlement and started to build homes. Seeing that the Pilgrims were weakened from the long winter and short on supplies, Squanto began teaching them how to live in the new land. He showed them how to trap eels, where to catch fish, and how to plant corn.

Squanto helped the Pilgrims in other ways, too. He spoke English well, since he had been kidnapped and taken to live in England for a number of years. Squanto used this knowledge to help the Pilgrims communicate and live peacefully with the Native Americans. Without Squanto, the colony might not have survived.

From Squanto's actions, what can you tell about the kind of person he was?

_____

_____

_____

• •

After eating his sandwich in record time, Paul dipped into his bag for a second one. "Oh boy," he thought to himself. "I'm starving. I guess I shouldn't have skipped breakfast. I could eat four or five sandwiches." Just as he started to tear the plastic wrap off the sandwich, Paul spotted Miranda. She wasn't eating because she had forgotten her lunch. "Hey, Miranda," Paul called. "Have a sandwich. I've already had one. It's your favorite—peanut butter and cherry jam."

From his actions, what can you tell about the kind of person Paul is?

_____

_____

_____

Read each article. Underline the correct answers.

Teacher Donna Valentine might teach her class in New York one day. The next day the class might be in Philadelphia or Boston. Sometimes, her class might be in another country altogether. Donna Valentine works for a circus. Her job is to teach young performers and the children of adult performers. Wherever the circus goes, Donna travels with it.

Young people often dream of joining a circus. Donna, though, didn't decide to work for the circus until her four children were grown. It was a good decision for Donna because she loves her job. She says her students are obedient and eager to learn. Another positive thing about the job is the opportunity it gives Donna to see the world. And, of course, she can see the circus just about anytime she wants.

1. **What makes Donna Valentine's teaching job easy?**
   A. Her students want to learn.
   B. Her students know more than regular students.
   C. Her students have extra time to study.
   D. Her students do a lot of traveling.

2. **Donna Valentine seems to be the kind of person who _____.**
   A. likes to stay in the same place
   B. likes to be by herself
   C. enjoys changes
   D. is proud of her home

• •

Do you hate hearing your alarm clock go off? Does its loud buzz irritate you? You may be interested in learning about a new kind of alarm. It doesn't use buzzers, bells, music, or flashing lights to wake up sleepers. Instead, it uses smells. When the alarm is set to go off, it sprays perfume into the air. The perfume could smell like flowers, hot coffee, or even chocolate candy. The inventors of the alarm believe it is a soothing way to get people out of bed in the morning.

Which one of the following groups of people would most likely buy the new alarm?
   A. people who hear better than most
   B. people who cannot hear
   C. people who work at night
   D. people who are light sleepers

24

Making Inferences About Fables

In a *fable*, an author tries to teach a lesson. Each story below is an example. As you read each fable in this section, try to infer the author's lesson.

Read the fables. Underline the best answer to each question.

Long, long ago, swans could sing. Then one day, they heard some horses neigh. The swans thought the sound of the horses' neighing was the loveliest sound they had ever heard. Right then, the swans stopped singing and tried neighing. They never did learn how to neigh, and in time they forgot how to sing.

What is the author trying to teach?

  A. Don't be jealous of others, for you may have more than they do.

  B. Share whatever you have with others.

  C. Don't worry about becoming famous.

  D. Don't give up your special abilities by trying to be like someone else.

The answer is *D*. The swans tried to neigh as the horses did and ended up losing their ability to sing. *A* is not correct. The fable does not suggest that the swans were jealous. *B* is not the best answer, either, because the fable doesn't talk about sharing with others. And *C* is not corrrect because the fable does not say anything about becoming famous.

• •

Dying of thirst, the crow was unable to find water anywhere. Finally, it spied a pitcher. There was water deep down inside the pitcher, but the crow couldn't reach it with its beak. The bird tried to break the pitcher, but it didn't succeed. Then it noticed some pebbles lying around. The crow began putting the pebbles into the pitcher. The water gradually rose. At last, it was high enough for the crow to reach.

What is the author trying to teach?

  A. Don't be too hasty or give up too soon.

  B. Serious problems often lead to clever ways of solving them.

  C. It is almost impossible to chase away thirsty crows.

  D. Be prepared for whatever life may bring you.

The answer is *B*. The crow was badly in need of water and thought of a clever way to get it. Often, our minds work best when we have to solve an important problem. Answers *A*, *C*, and *D* are not correct. The crow in the story wasn't hasty. No one tried to chase it away. And there was no mention of being prepared.

Teaching Lesson: Inferring a Fable's Lesson

Read the fables. Underline the best answer to each question.

A fox was walking through the forest when it spotted a boar. The boar was sharpening its tusks by rubbing them against the trunk of a tree. "Why are you sharpening your tusks?" the fox asked. "There are no hunters around, and there is no danger in sight."

The boar wisely answered, "I won't have time to sharpen my tusks when danger is near."

What is the author trying to teach?

   A. The fox is not as wise an animal as some people think.

   B. Prepare for danger before it comes.

   C. Sometimes people waste time by doing things in a hurry.

   D. Wise people are never lazy.

• •

The hungry fox licked its lips as it spotted clusters of juicy grapes hanging overhead. Stretching as high as it could, the fox still could not reach the grapes. Jumping didn't help, either. Finally, the fox gave up. As it slunk away, the fox said, "The grapes look ripe, but they are probably sour."

What is the author trying to teach?

   A. Greedy people are sometimes left with nothing.

   B. People's eyes are easily fooled, especially when it comes to food.

   C. If at first you don't succeed, try, try again.

   D. People sometimes criticize things they can't have.

• •

One day, a man and a lion were walking down a road through the forest. Each was bragging about his strength. While the two were boasting, they passed a large stone statue in a clearing. It was of a man wrestling with a lion. The man was winning.

Pointing to the statue, the man said, "You can see that men are stronger than lions."

"Aha!" replied the lion. "The statue was carved by a man. If it had been carved by a lion, the lion would be winning."

What is the author trying to teach?

   A. People see things from their own point of view.

   B. Bragging accomplishes nothing.

   C. Those who are not brave often say they are.

   D. People like others to think that they are stronger or braver than they really are.

Inferring a Fable's Lesson

Read the fables. Underline the best answer to each question.

A hungry dog crawled into the barn and lay by the hay. Snarling and barking, the jealous dog wouldn't let the horses in, even though the hay had been spread on the floor for them to eat. "He is a wicked dog," whinnied one of the horses. "He can't eat hay and is starving, but he won't let us have it either."

What is the author trying to teach?
- A. Try to see the good things that others do.
- B. Jealousy has ruined many a friendship.
- C. Through jealousy, others can be harmed needlessly.
- D. Always share what you have with those in need.

An eagle dove down from high in the sky and snatched up a lamb with its sharp talons. The eagle flew away with the lamb. A bird called a jackdaw saw what the eagle had done and wanted to do the same. The jackdaw flew onto the back of a ram. Its claws became tangled in the ram's thick wool, and the bird couldn't fly off.

A shepherd ran to the jackdaw and clipped its wings so it could never fly away. He gave the bird to his children. "What kind of bird is this?" the children asked.

"It's a jackdaw," replied the shepherd, "but it thinks it's an eagle."

What is the author trying to teach?
- A. Don't pick on someone bigger than you.
- B. Trying to be something you aren't can get you into trouble.
- C. Danger never seems to be very far away from the weak.
- D. Protect your freedom with your life.

The astronomer roamed about studying the stars each night. One evening, while he was walking just outside of town, he fell into a deep well. Bruised and cut, he cried out for help. Running to his aid, a stranger asked what had happened. Upon hearing the astronomer's story, the stranger remarked, "Why is it that you study the stars when you don't know what's here on earth?"

What is the author trying to teach?
- A. Don't roam around unfamiliar places after dark without a light.
- B. Don't get so lost in thought that you don't know what's going on around you.
- C. Beware of strangers, especially when you are in need of help.
- D. You can't always rely on others for help.

Read each article. Underline the correct answer to each question.

One day a scientist knocked over a bottle in his lab. The bottle fell to the floor and broke, but it didn't fall apart. The scientist couldn't believe his eyes. Carefully, he examined the bottle to discover why it had kept its shape. A chemical in the bottle had formed a rubbery coating that kept the broken pieces of glass together.

The scientist got an idea for making a new kind of glass. In time, safety glass was made using layers of plastic and glass. Unlike regular glass, safety glass does not fly all over if it is broken. There is no telling how many injuries have been prevented because of this kind of glass.

1. **What gave the scientist the idea for safety glass?**
   A. a series of carefully planned experiments
   B. accidentally breaking a bottle
   C. the work of other scientists
   D. a problem he had been trying to solve

2. **How did the scientist feel when he saw that the broken bottle had not come apart?**
   A. worried   B. happy   C. surprised   D. impatient

- -

Tom English was visiting a blind friend in the hospital when the friend began asking questions. "What would happen to me if a fire broke out in the hospital?" the friend asked. "How would I know where the exit is? Would someone remember to come and assist me?"

English thought about his friend's questions for a long time. He then made a new kind of exit sign. It was a talking sign that would be triggered by smoke or heat from a fire. The sign might say, "Fire in the building. Exit this way, please." As the fire got closer, the sign would talk louder and louder. The sign could also sense if fire was on the other side of the exit door. If it was, the sign would direct people to take a different exit.

1. **When Tom English visited his friend, how did the blind man feel?**
   A. angry   B. anxious   C. sick   D. sad

2. **If fire broke out and the exit sign talked very loudly, what would you know about the fire?**
   A. The fire was almost out.
   B. The fire was a big one.
   C. The fire was close to the sign.
   D. The fire department was on its way.

Read each article. Underline the correct answers.

Insects respond in various ways when they are attacked. Some fight back, and some play dead. Others pull in their legs and heads so they look like seeds. One insect, though, doesn't do anything when it is captured. It's the bella moth.

The bella moth feeds on poisonous plants. The poison doesn't hurt the moth, but it stays in the moth's body and can kill other creatures. The poison also makes the moth taste terrible. If a bella moth gets caught in a spider's web, the spider picks it up and tosses it out. The bella moth just flies away.

1. **Why doesn't the bella moth do anything when it is captured?**
    A. It can't fight very well.
    B. It is a slow flyer.
    C. It seems to know it will be set free.
    D. It gets tired easily.

2. **Why would an insect make itself look like a seed?**
    A. so birds wouldn't bother it
    B. so creatures that eat insects wouldn't think it is one
    C. so it could roll away to safety
    D. to make itself look better than other insects

• •

In some crowded parts of Asia, there are many people who live on houseboats. Often, there are so many houseboats that they form a town. The same water that keeps the houseboat afloat is also used for cooking, washing, and fishing. Where do the people go shopping? They shop there on the water. Store boats sail up and down the waterways selling food, clothes, tools, furniture, and anything else the people need.

1. **Why do you think these people live on boats?**
    A. They can take trips more easily.
    B. Jobs are easier to get.
    C. The land is very crowded
    D. They can catch fish for food.

2. **From the article, you can conclude that _____.**
    A. the people are poor and can't afford to live anywhere else
    B. the people spend most of their time on the houseboats
    C. the boats are small but sturdy
    D. there are few storms in that part of Asia

Read the ad. Underline the correct answers.

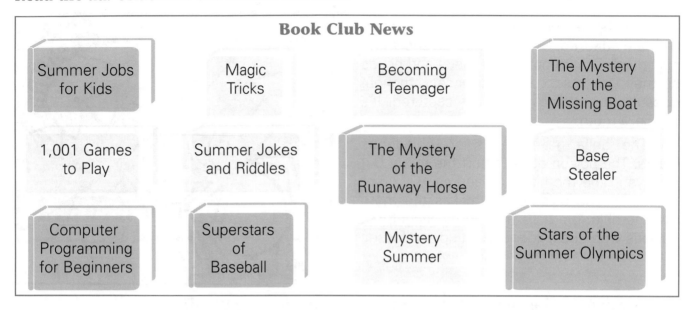

Book Club News

Summer Jobs for Kids

Magic Tricks

Becoming a Teenager

The Mystery of the Missing Boat

1,001 Games to Play

Summer Jokes and Riddles

The Mystery of the Runaway Horse

Base Stealer

Computer Programming for Beginners

Superstars of Baseball

Mystery Summer

Stars of the Summer Olympics

1. **When do you think this ad most likely appeared?**
   A. September or October
   B. November or December
   C. January or February
   D. April or May

2. **The ad was probably written for _____.**
   A. older teens getting ready for college
   B. very young children just learning to read
   C. young people who are about twelve years old
   D. older people, ages 50 and over

3. **Most of the books are about _____.**
   A. sports, hobbies, or mysteries
   B. jokes and riddles
   C. problems of growing up
   D. games

4. **Raffie and his friends sometimes run out of things to do. Which book might they choose?**
   A. *Base Stealer*
   B. *Runaway Horse*
   C. *1,001 Games to Play*
   D. *Stars of the Summer Olympics*

5. **Alicia enjoys books about animals and mysteries. Which book would she most likely choose?**
   A. *Mystery Summer*
   B. *The Mystery of the Runaway Horse*
   C. *The Mystery of the Missing Boat*
   D. *Magic Tricks*

Read each article. Underline the best answers.

The Plains tribes of North America lived in large tentlike homes called tepees (also spelled *tipis*). A typical tepee was made of fifteen buffalo hides carefully sewn together. Wooden poles held the tent up and stretched out the skins. The home was about 18 feet high and 14 feet wide in the middle. Despite its large size, the tent could be put up or taken down in 30 minutes.

1. **Tepees were especially good for tribes that _____.**

   A. stayed in one place   C. moved from place to place

   B. lived near towns   D. had small farms

2. **Native Americans of the Plains were probably _____.**

   A. farmers   B. hunters   C. sheep herders   D. cattle ranchers

• •

Victorville, California, has the largest solar-cell factory in the world. A person arriving in Victorville sees a strange sight—row after row of panels covered with circles of glass. Observing the panels closely, one would see all 108 panels turn slightly. Tiny motors turn the panels so they face the sun from sunrise to sunset. The cells in the panels turn the sun's light into electricity. The panels make enough electricity for 400 homes, and they don't use oil, gas, wood, or coal. Nor do they pollute the air.

Solar-cell panels are costly to construct. Once they're built, however, they cost next to nothing to run and require very little care. As companies produce more and more panels, they will find cheaper ways to make them. The price should go down just about every year.

1. **Solar panels would work best in _____.**

   A. places where the weather changes frequently

   B. places that have an average amount of rainfall

   C. desertlike, sunny places

   D. hilly places

2. **Why do you think solar-cell panels haven't been used very much?**

   A. There aren't many places where they can be put.

   B. They break down frequently.

   C. Other ways of making electricity are still cheaper.

   D. The electric companies don't want to change their ways.

Inferring the Author's Purpose

Authors have different purposes for writing. Those who write schoolbooks or encyclopedias are trying to give you information or explain how things work. They want you to learn from what they have written. Authors who write stories, poems, or plays are trying to entertain you. They want you to enjoy what they have written. Authors who write advertisements and editorials are trying to persuade you. They want you to buy a product, vote for a particular person, or lend your support to a plan or idea.

Authors can have more than one purpose. They may want to both inform and entertain you. And authors who write stories may hope that you learn something, too. But usually, authors have just one main purpose.

Read the article. Underline the best answer.

Alfredo wanted his lunch counter to be special. Instead of selling the usual foods such as fries and hamburgers, he wanted to sell healthy foods: steaming home-cooked soup on cold days, ice-cold lemonade and limeade on hot days. Of course, all that would be only a dream unless he got the loan to open his lunch counter. Just then there was a knock at the door. It was the mail carrier with a registered letter. Alfredo didn't know it then, but his dream was about to come true.

The author's main purpose in writing this passage was to _____.

   A. persuade people to eat healthy food because it's better for them
   B. explain what must be done to start a new business
   C. entertain readers with a story about a man starting a business
   D. give information about healthy foods for winter and summer

Did you underline *C?* If so, you are correct. The author is telling a story about a man who wants to start a lunch counter business. Even though some information is given about what it takes to start a business, the author's main purpose here is to entertain.

Read each article. Underline the best answers.

Tired of sugary soft drinks? Are you looking for a drink that tastes good and is good for you? Try Lenora's Limeade. It's a refreshingly different drink. And it's loaded with vitamin C.

The author's main purpose in writing this passage was to _____.
   A. persuade people to buy limeade
   B. explain why limeade is good for you
   C. explain how limeade is made
   D. entertain you with an interesting story

> Did you underline *A?* If so, you are correct. The article describes Lenora's Limeade as tasting good and being good for you. The author is trying to persuade you to buy it.

• •

Limes once saved lives. Years ago, sailors were often struck by a strange disease called scurvy. Their teeth would fall out, and their gums would bleed. They wouldn't feel like eating, and they would become thin and weak. If the disease got bad enough, they would die. One ship's captain lost 60 of his 160 men to this disease.

Scurvy is caused by a lack of vitamin C. Vitamin C is found in citrus fruits—lemons, limes, oranges, and grapefruit—and green vegetables. Because they weren't getting fresh fruits or vegetables, sailors often developed scurvy on long voyages. In 1795, the English Navy began giving its sailors a lime each day. That put an end to scurvy among British sailors.

The author's main purpose in writing this passage was to _____.
   A. persuade people to eat limes to keep their teeth clean
   B. explain how limes were used to prevent scurvy
   C. entertain readers with a story about the English Navy
   D. give information about the English Navy

> Did you underline *B?* If so, you are correct. The article describes scurvy and how limes, and other sources of vitamin C, can prevent it. The author's main purpose is to explain how a serious disease was prevented.

Read each article. Underline the best answers.

Making cheese takes a lot of milk. In fact, it takes 11 pounds of milk to make a single pound of cheese. In making cheese, the first step is to heat the milk to kill any harmful germs that might be in it. Bacteria are then mixed into the milk. Bacteria are tiny bits of living matter. They separate the solid part of the milk (the curd) from the liquid part (the whey). The milk begins to turn sour. A natural chemical called rennet extract is then added. This causes the milk to curdle, which means that the milk thickens. The milk is stirred with large paddles and heated to evaporate some of the whey. After the remaining whey is drained off, the curd is placed in molds and put in a curing room. Depending on the kind of cheese being made, it is left there for anywhere from a few weeks to two years. The longer it is left in the curing room, the sharper the taste.

The author's main purpose in writing this passage was to _____.
- A. persuade people to eat cheese
- B. explain how cheese is made
- C. tell a story to entertain readers
- D. tell why cheese is good for you

• •

Things taste better with cheese. Add cheese to your next hamburger to create a taste-tempting cheeseburger. Add a sprinkling of grated cheese to your favorite salad. Pour melted cheese on broccoli and cauliflower to perk up their flavor. Take a tip from the Association of Cheese Makers. Cheese makes your favorite foods taste even better.

The author's main purpose in writing this passage was to _____.
- A. persuade people to eat cheese
- B. list all the ways cheese may be used
- C. tell an interesting story
- D. tell why cheese is good for you

• •

Fred refused to eat any food but cheeseburgers. "O.K.," said the camp counselor. "Cheeseburgers it is!" For the next three weeks, Fred ate nothing but cheeseburgers. By then, he was sick of them. Even broccoli was starting to look good. But Fred had made such a big fuss about eating nothing but cheeseburgers. How could he admit that he had been wrong?

The author's main purpose in writing this passage was to _____.
- A. persuade people to eat cheeseburgers
- B. explain how to cook cheeseburgers
- C. amuse readers with an interesting story
- D. inform people that it is important to eat a variety of foods

Inferring Author's Purpose

Read each article. Underline the best answers.

The skin that covers your body today isn't the same skin that you had three weeks ago. Old skin is constantly being replaced by new skin. Every three weeks you end up with a completely new coat of skin.

Skin is made up of two layers: the dermis and the epidermis. The dermis is the bottom or inner layer. The epidermis is the top or outer layer. Skin is made up of millions of tiny body parts known as cells. New cells are formed at the bottom of the dermis and gradually move upward. Within three weeks, they will move up and replace the dermis.

The surface of the skin is covered with dead cells. Millions of these dead cells are washed away every time you take a bath or shower. In fact, even as you read this article, dead cells are flaking off your body. In a day's time you will lose more than 50 million cells. However, these cells will be immediately replaced by cells just under your skin's surface.

The author's main purpose in writing this passage was to _____.

  A. persuade people to keep their skin clean

  B. explain how skin changes

  C. amuse readers with an interesting story

  D. sell a certain kind of soap

• •

Are your hands coated with stubborn ink stains? Do you have grease beneath your fingernails? Clean your hands as they have never been cleaned before. Use Sand Hand Cleaner. Guaranteed to get your hands their cleanest!

The author's main purpose in writing this passage was to _____.

  A. persuade people to keep their skin clean

  B. explain why some hand cleaners work better than others

  C. tell an interesting story

  D. sell a certain kind of soap

• •

Jack was lying. The detective was sure of that. He had claimed to be a carpenter. But when they shook hands, he noticed that Jack's hands were smooth and soft. If he were a carpenter, his hands would be rough and callused from using tools.

The author's main purpose in writing this passage was to _____.

  A. persuade people to take care of their hands

  B. explain how a detective catches a criminal

  C. entertain readers with an interesting story

  D. sell a certain kind of carpenter's tools

Using Context Clues to Infer Word Meanings

Read the following brief paragraph. Notice how the boldfaced words are used. See if you can infer what each word means.

President Clinton is one of our most **loquacious** presidents. He loves to talk. Many visitors to the White House say that President Clinton would talk to them hour after hour. Calvin Coolidge, on the other hand, was **taciturn**. He seemed to have little to say.

According to one story, a dinner guest told President Coolidge that a friend had bet him he couldn't get the president to say more than two words. Looking the dinner guest straight in the eye, Coolidge replied, "You lose."

> Can you tell from the ways that the words are used in the article that **loquacious** means *talkative* and **taciturn** means *quiet?* To infer the meaning of an unknown word, see how the word is used in the sentence and in the whole passage. Look for clues that will help you guess the meaning of the word. For instance, the article says that Clinton is **loquacious**. Then it says that he loves to talk. You can guess that **loquacious** means *talkative*. By using a contrast, the article also gives clues that **taciturn** means the opposite, or *quiet*.
>
> To check on the meaning you have inferred, substitute your guess for the hard word. See if it fits and makes sense. When you substitute *talkative* for **loquacious** and *quiet* for **taciturn**, you can see that they fit in with what the article is saying.

Using context clues, try to guess the meaning of each boldfaced word in the following article. Underline the best answers.

One of the trickiest animals is the squid. If attacked, it shoots out a cloud of ink. This makes the squid hard to see, and it also makes the animal harder to smell. Attackers have a difficult time using both their sense of sight and their **olfactory** sense to find the squid. One kind of squid shoots out its ink in such a way that it forms the shape of a squid. The attacking animal will **pursue** the ink shape rather than the real thing.

1. **As used in the article, the word *olfactory* means _____.**

   A. having to do with the sense of smell   C. having to do with the sense of touch

   B. having to do with the sense of sight   D. having to do with the sense of hearing

> Did you select *A?* If so, you are correct. The article says that the cloud of ink makes the squid hard to see and smell. Then it says that "attackers have a difficult time using both their sense of sight and their **olfactory** sense." Thinking about both these sentences, you can see that **olfactory** has to do with the sense of smell.

2. **As used in the article, the word *pursue* means _____.**

   A. go after   B. lose   C. put away   D. sink

Teaching Lesson: Inferring Word Meanings

Using context clues, try to guess the meaning of each boldfaced word in the following articles. Underline the best answers.

In bowling, it isn't easy to get a strike. You have to knock down all 10 pins at once. But now and again, some really good bowlers roll a perfect game. Impossible as it seems, they get 10 strikes in a row for a score of 300. One day in February 1997, a 20-year-old college student by the name of Jeremy Sonnefeld did even better than that. What's better than a perfect game? Three perfect games. **Incredibly,** Jeremy rolled 30 strikes in a row for a total score of 900. That's like a baseball pitcher throwing three no-hitters in a row. The

National Bowling Congress has been keeping records for 101 years. In all that time, no one has ever officially bowled three perfect games.

What did Sonnefeld have to say about his amazing **feat?** "Luck has a lot to do with it," he commented. "You can throw a shot that is perfect, and then have one pin standing." He added, "To bowl 30 strikes in a row is unthinkable." Even he had a hard time believing that he had actually bowled three perfect games.

1. **As used in the article, the word *incredibly* means _____.**

    A. quickly   B. silently   C. officially   D. unbelievably

2. **As used in the article, the word *feat* means _____.**

    A. great or difficult act or deed   C. costly gift

    B. something we walk on   D. a planned happening

• •

Suppose you are a young person looking for a job in England in the 1700s. You hear stories about America, and you know that good workers are badly needed there. You would like to go to America, but you have no money to pay for passage on a sailing ship. How can you get there? One way is by becoming an indentured servant. As an indentured servant, you agree to work for a family for 4 to 7 years. In return, the family **reimburses** the sailing ship company for your passage. During those 4 to 7 years, you are given food and a place to stay, but no money.

And you can't leave and go to work for someone else, even if you don't like the family or the work they give you. After your time as an indentured servant is up, the person you worked for might give you a little money, some clothes, and a small piece of land.

In those early days, even criminals were sometimes given the choice of going to prison in England or to America as indentured servants. The practice of using indentured servants was halted in the 1820s. By that time there was an **abundance** of willing workers streaming into the United States.

1. **As used in the article, the word *reimburses* means _____.**

    A. pays money to   C. promises to pay

    B. owes money to   D. borrows money from

2. **As used in the article, the word *abundance* means _____.**

    A. news   B. talk   C. plenty   D. plans

Inferring Word Meanings

Using context clues, try to guess the meaning of each boldfaced word in the following articles. Underline the best answers.

Many years ago, Hiawatha became a leader of the Mohawk tribe. Tired of all the fighting among the tribes and sickened by the senseless killing, Hiawatha spoke out for peace. He thought that the tribes should help each other. When Hiawatha's wife and children were killed by cruel warriors, Hiawatha was overcome by **grief.** He built a lodge of tree branches in the forest. He wanted to be away from everyone. After many months had passed, Hiawatha was approached by Degandawida, who was a member of the Huron tribe. Known as the Peacemaker, Degandawida was a kindly man. He persuaded Hiawatha to return to his people and speak out for peace. The two men drew up a plan. The five tribes would join together in a **federation.** Each tribe would send ten chiefs to meetings that would be held in an Onondaga village. Disagreements would be settled by this council of chiefs. Hiawatha and Degandawida also wrote a set of rules for the Iroquois federation. The plan worked well. With the help of the federation, the tribes lived together in peace.

1. **As used in the article, the word *grief* means _____.**
   A. sorrow
   B. loneliness
   C. anger
   D. happiness

2. **As used in the article, the word *federation* means _____.**
   A. an important meeting
   B. a set of rules
   C. a large celebration
   D. a group of tribes, states, or nations

• •

It looked like the end of the war. In the winter of 1776, Americans were fighting for their independence, though losing battle after battle to the better-trained British armies. General Washington and his army had barely escaped being captured in New Jersey. **Fleeing** for their lives from General Cornwallis, they sailed across the Delaware River to Pennsylvania. They took all the boats with them so the British couldn't follow.

Then the British made a **grave** mistake. Instead of taking advantage of their victories, they set up a series of winter camps. Meanwhile, Washington formed a daring plan. While the Hessians, German soldiers paid to fight for the British, were celebrating Christmas, Washington and his men crossed back over the icy Delaware. They marched toward Trenton where the Hessians had set up camp. At 8:00 A.M. on December 26, the Americans surprised the Hessians and captured the camp. Washington's daring deed put new life in America's fight for freedom.

1. **As used in the article, the word *fleeing* means _____.**
   A. fighting
   B. supplying
   C. worrying
   D. running

2. **As used in the article, the word *grave* means _____.**
   A. serious
   B. funny
   C. cowardly
   D. confusing

Teaching Lesson: Inferring Feelings

Using context clues, try to guess the meaning of each boldfaced word in the following articles. Underline the best answers.

Robots have been used in factories to **assemble** cars, TVs, and other products. Now robots can go places that are too dangerous for people. A robot by the name of Dante II has been sent inside a volcano. Ten feet tall and ten feet long, Dante walks on eight legs like some sort of giant metal crab. Using **advanced** computer sensors that detect objects in front of it, Dante can walk over or around large boulders, avoid stepping into holes, and make its way down steep slopes. In 1994, Dante crawled nearly 700 feet down the slope of a volcano in Alaska. At the bottom of the crater, Dante gathered information about heat and gases created by an erupting volcano. Because it was giving off poisonous gases and could erupt without warning, the volcano was too dangerous for humans to enter.

Robots like Dante will also be used to study the ocean. And Sojourner, a specially built little robot, was sent to Mars to gather information. Its movements across the rocky Martian terrain fascinated people on Earth.

1. As used in the article, the word *assemble* means _____.
   A. protect   B. put together   C. sell   D. fix

2. As used in the article, the word *advanced* means _____.
   A. in front of   C. first in line
   B. having lived a great many years   D. beyond others in what it can do

• •

In 1848, gold was discovered in California. By 1849, thousands of people had rushed there hoping to get rich. But only a few hundred miners found enough gold to become wealthy. The **majority** found no gold at all. However, some people learned that there were other ways to become rich. They sold things to the miners. Because of the gold rush, prices were **inflated.** A dozen eggs could be sold for $10. A slice of bread might cost a dollar.

A man named Philip Armour opened a small meat shop in Placerville. Using the money he made there, he built one of the country's largest meat-packing businesses. John Studebaker made money selling wheelbarrows. When the gold rush was over, he went back to South Bend, Indiana. He put his money into a company that sold horse-drawn wagons. Later, Studebaker's company manufactured cars. And Studebaker became very rich.

1. As used in the article, the word *majority* means _____.
   A. greatest number; more than half   C. those who came late; stragglers
   B. most important; best known   D. those who worked the least; slackers

2. As used in the article, the word *inflated* means _____.
   A. higher than they should have been   C. clearly marked
   B. full of air   D. changing from one day to the next

Making Inferences About Stories

When you read a story, you make lots of inferences, for example, about feelings and character traits. These inferences have already been discussed in this book. However, you might also need to infer the story's setting. The setting tells where and when the story took place. Sometimes the author does not directly tell what the setting is. If there are lots of people around and tall buildings, though, you can infer that the story is taking place in a city. If the people are in horse-drawn wagons, you can infer that the story took place a hundred years ago or more.

You might also want to draw a conclusion about the type of story that you're reading. Study the chart below that shows the different types of stories, or *genres*.

GENRE	DESCRIPTION
Fantasy	Fantasy stories tell about events that could not happen, or about people or other creatures that could not exist. **Example:** a story about a girl who can fly
Folktale	Folktales are usually old stories that have been handed down over the years. They may include magic or feature animals that act like people. Often, there is a lesson to be learned. Folktales include fairy tales, fables, tall tales, legends, and myths. **Examples:** a story about a hero who is turned into a frog by an evil magician, or a mouse who helps a lion
Realistic fiction	People and events in a story seem true to life. **Example:** a story about a sixth-grader who faces problems trying to make the soccer team
Science fiction	Advances in science and technology are an important part of the story. **Example:** a story about teens traveling into the 25th century
Mystery	Crimes are solved or puzzling events are explained. **Example:** a story about a girl detective who solves the mystery of some missing books
Biography	The story of a real person's life is told by another person. **Example:** a story about Abraham Lincoln

The following selection has been taken from *Gulliver's Travels* by Jonathan Swift. Lemuel Gulliver was a doctor aboard a sailing ship. After his boat sank, Gulliver swam for shore. This is his story in his own words. Read the story. Then underline or write the answer to each question.

Voyage to Lilliput: Part One

I swam as fortune directed me, and was pushed forward by wind and tide. But when I was able to struggle no longer I found myself within my depth. By this time the storm had much abated. I reached the shore at last, about eight o'clock in the evening, and advanced nearly half a mile inland, but could not discover any sign of houses or inhabitants. I was extremely tired. I found myself much inclined to sleep. I lay down on the grass and slept sounder than ever I did in my life for above nine hours.

When I awakened, it was just daylight. I attempted to rise, but was not able to stir. For as I happened to be lying on my back, I found my arms and legs were strongly fastened on each side to the ground. My hair, which was long and thick, was tied down in the same manner. I could only look upwards. The sun began to grow hot, and the light hurt my eyes. I heard a confused noise about me, but could see nothing except the sky. In a little time I felt something alive moving on my left leg. It advanced gently over my chest and came almost up to my chin. Bending my eyes downward, I saw it was a human creature, not six inches high. In the meantime I felt at least forty more following the first. I was in the utmost astonishment, and roared so loud that they all ran back in a fright. However, they soon returned. One of them, who ventured so far as to get a full sight of my face, cried out in a shrill voice, "Hekinah Degul!" The others repeated the same words several times, but I then knew not what they meant.

I lay all this while in great uneasiness. But at length, struggling to get loose, I succeeded in breaking the strings that fastened my left arm to the ground. At the same time, with a violent pull that gave me extreme pain, I a little loosened the strings that tied down my hair,

so that I was just able to turn my head about two inches. But the creatures ran off a second time before I could seize them. There was a great shout, and in an instant I felt about a hundred arrows discharged on my left hand, which hurt like so many needles. Moreover, they shot another flight into the air, of which some fell on my face, which I immediately covered with my left hand. When this shower of arrows was over, I groaned with grief and pain, and then, because I was striving again to get loose, they discharged another flight of arrows larger than the first.

By this time I thought it most **prudent** to lie still till night, when, my left hand being already loose, I could easily free myself. As for the inhabitants, I thought I might be a match for the greatest army they could bring against me if they were all of the same size with him I saw. When the people observed that I was quiet they discharged no more arrows. By the noise I heard I knew that their number was increased. About four yards from me, for more than an hour, there was a knocking, like people at work. Turning my head, I saw a stage set up, about a foot and a half from the ground, with two or three ladders to mount it.

After some time, there appeared before me a person of high rank from his imperial majesty. I made a sign to signify that I wanted liberty. It appeared that he understood me well enough, for he shook his head to show his disapproval. It seems that upon the first moment I was discovered sleeping on the ground after my landing, the emperor had ordered that I be tied and that a machine be sent to carry me to the capital city. Five hundred carpenters and engineers had been set at work to prepare the greatest engine they had. It was a frame of wood, raised three inches from the ground, about seven feet long and four wide, moving upon twenty-two wheels. But the difficulty was to lace me on it. Eighty poles were erected for this purpose, and very strong cords fastened to bandages which the workmen had tied round my neck, hands, body, and legs. Nine hundred of the strongest men were employed to draw up these cords by pulleys fastened on the poles, and in less than three hours I was raised and slung into the engine, and there tied fast. Fifteen hundred of the emperor's largest horses, each about four inches and a half high, were then employed to draw me towards the capital.

Where the carriage stopped there stood an ancient building, supposed to be the largest in the whole kingdom, and here it was determined that I should lodge. Near the great gate, through which I could easily creep, they fixed ninety-one chains, like those which hang to a lady's watch. They were locked to my left leg with thirty-six padlocks. When the workmen found it was impossible for me to break loose, they cut all the strings that bound me. Then I rose up, feeling as melancholy as ever I did in my life. The chains that held my left leg were about two yards long, and gave me not only freedom to walk backwards and forwards in a semicircle, but to creep in and lie at full length inside the great building.

1. **Where does the story take place?**
   A. in England
   B. in South America
   C. in an imaginary land of little people
   D. on a newly discovered continent

2. **What is the story problem?**
   A. Gulliver is hungry.
   B. Gulliver is lost.
   C. Gulliver has been captured.
   D. Gulliver is afraid of the Lilliputians.

3. **In its present form, this story could best be described as being _____.**
   A. realistic fiction
   B. fantasy
   C. biography
   D. mystery

4. **As used in the story, the word *prudent* means _____.**
   A. clever
   B. angry
   C. wise
   D. hopeful

5. **What clues in the story tell you that it takes place many years ago?**

   _____

   _____

   _____

6. **What do you predict will happen in the next part of the story?**

   _____

   _____

   _____

Making Inferences About Stories

Read part two of the story. Then underline or write the answer to each question.

Voyage to Lilliput: Part Two

The emperor looked at me with great admiration, but kept beyond the length of my chain. He was taller by about the breadth of my nail than any of his court, which alone was enough to strike awe into the beholders, and graceful and majestic. The better to behold him, I lay down on my side, so that my face was level with his, and he stood three yards off. However, I have had him since many times in my hand. His dress was very simple; but he wore a light helmet of gold, adorned with jewels and a plume. He held his sword in his hand, to defend himself if I should break loose. It was almost three inches long, and the hilt was of gold, enriched with diamonds. His voice was shrill, but very clear. His majesty spoke often to me, and I answered. But neither of us could understand a word.

Towards night I got with some difficulty into my house, where I lay on the ground, as I had to do for a fortnight, till a bed was prepared for me out of six hundred beds of the ordinary measure. Six hundred servants were appointed me, and three hundred tailors made me a suit of clothes. Moreover, six of his majesty's greatest scholars were employed to teach me their language, so that soon I was able to converse after a fashion with the emperor. The first words I learned were to desire that he would please to give me my liberty, which I every day repeated on my knees. But he answered that this must be a work of time, and that first I must swear a peace with him and his kingdom.

Through my gentleness and good behavior, I hoped to obtain my freedom. The people came by degrees to be less fearful of me. I would sometimes lie down and let five or six dance in my hand. And at last the boys and girls ventured to come and play at hide-and-seek in my hair.

I had sent so many **petitions** for my liberty that his majesty at length mentioned the matter in a full council, where it was finally approved but with the following conditions.

First. The Man-Mountain shall not depart from our dominions without our license under the great seal.

Second. He shall not presume to come into our city without our express order, at which time the **inhabitants** shall have two hours' warning to keep within doors.

Third. The said Man-Mountain shall confine his walks to our principal high roads and not walk or lie down in a meadow or field of corn.

Fourth. As he walks the said roads, he shall take the utmost care not to trample upon any of our loving subjects, their horses, or carriages, nor take any of our subjects into his hands without their consent.

Fifth. If a message needs to be delivered with extraordinary speed, Man-Mountain shall be required to carry in his pocket horse and rider a six days' journey and return the said messenger (if so required) safe to our imperial presence.

Sixth. He shall be our ally against our enemies in the island of Blefuscu. He shall do his utmost to destroy their fleet, which is now preparing to invade us.

Lastly. Upon his solemn oath to observe all the above articles, the said Man-Mountain shall have a daily allowance of meat and drink sufficient for the support of 1,724 of our subjects.

I swore to these articles with great cheerfulness, whereupon my chains were removed, and I was at full liberty.

1. **What is the story problem in this part of the story?**
   A. Gulliver wishes to go home.
   B. Gulliver wants his freedom.
   C. Gulliver wants more food.
   D. Gulliver wants people to leave him alone.

2. **As used in the story, the word *petitions* means _____.**
   A. written requests   B. insults   C. messengers   D. costly gifts

3. **As used in the story, the word *inhabitants* means _____.**
   A. enemies
   B. best friends
   C. a country's army and navy
   D. people living in a place

4. **What is strange about the conditions that the emperor sets for Gulliver?**

   _____

   _____

   _____

5. **How do you know that Gulliver is a kindhearted person? Give examples.**

   _____

   _____

   _____

6. **What do you predict will happen in part three of the story?**

   _____

   _____

   _____

Making Inferences About Stories

Read part three of the story. Then underline the answers to the questions that follow.

Voyage to Lilliput: Part Three

Later, Gulliver promised to help the emperor in his war with Blefuscu. Ships from Blefuscu were already on their way to invade Lilliput.

It was not long before I communicated to his majesty the plan I had formed for **seizing** the enemy's whole fleet. The Empire of Blefuscu is an island parted from Lilliput only by a channel eight hundred yards wide. I **consulted** the most experienced seamen on the depth of the channel, and they told me that in the middle, at high water, it was seventy *glumgluffs* (about six feet of European measure). I walked towards the coast, where, lying down behind a hillock, I took out my spyglass, and viewed the enemy's fleet at anchor—about fifty men-of-war and other vessels. I then came back to the house and gave orders for a great quantity of the strongest cable and bars of iron. The cable was about as thick as packthread, and the bars of the length and size of a knitting-needle. I trebled the cable to make it stronger, and for the same reason twisted three of the iron bars together, bending the ends into a hook. Having thus fixed fifty hooks to as many cables, I went back to the coast, and taking off my coat, shoes, and stockings, walked into the sea in my leather jacket about half an hour before high water. I waded with what haste I could, swimming in the middle about thirty yards until I felt ground. Thus I arrived at the fleet in half an hour.

The enemy were so frightened when they saw me that they hopped out of their ships and swam for shore. Then, fastening a hook to the hole at the prow of each ship, I tied all the cords together at the end. Meanwhile, the enemy discharged several thousand arrows, many of which stuck in my hands and face. My greatest fear was for my eyes. I took out my spectacles and fastened them upon my nose. I went on with my work in spite of the arrows, many of which struck against the glasses of my spectacles, but without any other effect than slightly disturbing them.

Then taking the knot in my hand I began to pull. But not a ship would stir, for they were too fast held by their anchors. Letting go the cord, I cut with my knife the cables that held the anchors. Then I took up again the knotted end of the cables to which my hooks were tied. With great ease, I drew fifty of the enemy's men-of-war after me.

When the Blefuscudians saw the fleet moving in order, and me pulling at the end, they set up a scream of grief and despair that is impossible to describe. When I got out of danger I stopped awhile to pick out the arrows that stuck in my hands and face. I then took off my spectacles. After waiting an hour, till the tide was a little fallen, I waded into the royal port of Lilliput. About three weeks after this exploit there arrived an embassy from Blefuscu, with humble offers of peace, which was soon concluded, on terms very advantageous to our Emperor.

Later, Gulliver found a full-size boat. He set out for home and was picked up by a passing ship. The sailors didn't believe his tale of being in a land of little people until he reached in his pocket and pulled out some cattle that he had brought with him. Gulliver arrived home on April 13, 1702, but soon set off on another voyage.

1. **What is the story problem in this part of the story?**
   A. Guliver wants to escape from Lilliput.
   B. Gulliver is attacked by an enemy fleet.
   C. Gulliver is captured by Blefuscudians.
   D. Gulliver has to stop an enemy fleet from attacking Lilliput.

2. **As used in the story, the word *seizing* means _____.**
   A. grabbing   B. selling   C. discovering   D. pushing

3. **As used in the story, the word *consulted* means _____.**
   A. ordered   C. was friendly with
   B. got information from   D. asked permission

4. **How do you know that the Blefuscudians are afraid of Gulliver?**

   _____

   _____

   _____

5. **How do you know that the Blefuscudians were very upset when they saw Gulliver hauling their ships away?**

   _____

   _____

   _____

6. **How do you know that Gulliver is a clever person?**

   _____

   _____

   _____

Making Inferences About Stories

Read the following poem. Then underline the right answer to each question.

FROM A RAILWAY CARRIAGE
by Robert Louis Stevenson

Faster than fairies, faster than witches,
Bridges and houses, hedges and ditches;
And charging along like troops in a battle
All through the meadows the horses and cattle:
All of the sights of the hill and the plain
Fly as thick as driving rain;
And ever again, in the wink of an eye,
Painted stations whistle by.

Here is a child who clambers and scrambles,
All by himself and gathering brambles;
Here is a tramp who stands and gazes;
And there is the green for stringing the daisies!
Here is a cart run away in the road
Lumping along with man and load;
And here is a mill, and there is a river:
Each a glimpse and gone for ever.

1. **Where is the narrator and what is he doing?**
   A. on a train sleeping
   B. on a train looking out the window
   C. at home reading about trains
   D. outside watching a train fly by

2. **What is the narrator trying to say?**
   A. The outside world is flashing by.
   B. Traveling by train is more fun than traveling by plane.
   C. You can learn a lot by traveling.
   D. From a train, people look funny.

3. **Where is the train?**
   A. in a tunnel
   B. in the country
   C. on a bridge
   D. in a city

Making Inferences About Poems

Read the following poem. Then underline the right answer to each question.

TRAVEL
by Edna St. Vincent Millay

The railroad track is miles away,
    And the day is loud with voices speaking,
Yet there isn't a train goes by all day
    But I hear its whistle shrieking.

All night there isn't a train goes by,
    Though the night is still for sleep and dreaming
But I see its cinders red on the sky,
    And hear its engine steaming.

My heart is warm with the friends I make,
    And better friends I'll not be knowing,
Yet there isn't a train I wouldn't take,
    No matter where it's going.

1. **What does the narrator most want to do?**
   A. take a trip on a train
   B. visit friends
   C. make new friends
   D. get to know old friends better

2. **What suggests that this poem was written a long time ago?**
   A. Few people travel by train today.
   B. The train had a steam engine.
   C. The train was slow.
   D. The track was miles away.

3. **How do you know that the train was burning coal or wood?**
   A. The narrator sees red cinders.
   B. The train makes a lot of noise.
   C. The train is far away.
   D. The narrator says her heart is warm.

· ·

TAKING OFF

The airplane taxis down the field
And heads into the breeze,
It lifts its wheels above the ground,
It skims above the trees,
It rises high and higher
Away up toward the sun,
It's just a speck against the sky
—And now it's gone!

What did you like best about this poem? Write your answer on the lines.

_____

_____

_____

Making Inferences About Poems